EMMERDALE

Please drive carefully
through our village

£7.99

Emmerdale™

The Official Annual 2011

Written by Lance Parkin

itv STUDIOS

Design: Brian Thomson

Picture Research: Dave Woodward & David Crook

A Grange Publication

© 2010. Published by Grange Communications Ltd., Edinburgh, under licence from ITV Studios Global Entertainment Ltd. Printed in the EU.

ISBN 978-1-907104-83-1

08

Who's Who?

16

2010 Highlights

26

Woolpack Gossip

28

Happily Ever After?

32

The Loves of Cain Dingle

34

Heroes & Villains

36

Favourite Moments

**New Kids
on the Block**

CONTENTS

Who's Who? 8
2010 Highlights 16
A Family Affair 22
New Kids on the Block 24
Woolpack Gossip 26
Happily Ever After? 28
The Village 30
The Loves of Cain Dingle......................32
Heroes & Villains...................................34
Favourite Moments................................36
Headlines Quiz.......................................39
The King Dynasty 40
Wordsearch 43
Gone... But Not Forgotten 44
Where's Belle...48
Crossword 49
10 Facts About Cast Members.............50
Behind the Scenes 52
Disasters 54
The Big Quiz 57
Awards and Accolades 58
Quiz Answers...60
Heartthrobs 62

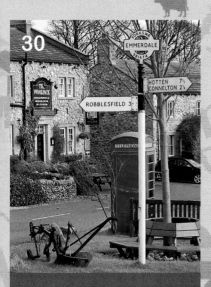

The Village

The King Dynasty

**Gone... But
Not Forgotten**

Disasters

WHO'S WHO?

Emmerdale is full of colourful characters, but most of the major events that happen in the village seem to revolve around a few large families. Over the years, individuals have come and gone, members of these clans have married each other, had children, feuded and fought. This is a quick introduction to who lives in Emmerdale these days, and how they're related.

THE SUGDENS

The Sugden family has worked the land at Emmerdale Farm for centuries. The village of Emmerdale used to be called Beckindale, but was renamed after the Sugden family farm in recognition of their importance.

The first episode of the series in 1972, started with the funeral of Jacob Sugden, owner of Emmerdale Farm. He left a widow, Annie (b 1920) and two sons, Jack and Joe.

Jack (1947 – 2009) was the eldest son, and so inherited the farm, even though he was an aspiring writer who wasn't interested in modern farming. He came to understand his duty, but remained committed to a respect for the land and was ahead of his time in terms of organic techniques and other 'green' issues. Joe (1949 – 1995) was often frustrated by his brother's idealism.

Annie

Jacob's Funeral

Joe

Sarah

Jack with Andy, Victoria-Anne and Robert

Jack's childhood sweetheart was Pat, and although he didn't know it for many years, she had his son, Jackie. Jack and Pat married in 1982, and had another son, Robert (b 1986). Pat died in a car crash soon after Robert was born. Jackie died in a gun accident a couple of years later.

Jack got married again, to Sarah (1952-2000). They had a daughter, VICTORIA-ANNE (b 1994) and adopted a son, ANDY (b 1986). Sarah was killed when Andy burned down a barn for the insurance money, not knowing his mother was inside. Andy had a half-brother, Daz Eden, who lived with him for a number of years (and who would have a brief relationship with Victoria).

Andy married KATIE Addyman (b 1986), although in the run up to the wedding she was already having an affair with his brother Robert. As his marriage fell apart, he was consoled by Debbie Dingle, who secretly had his daughter, SARAH (b 2005).

He started a relationship with Jo Stiles, they married but failed to adopt Sarah, and Jo left Andy because he'd become violent.

Katie

Andy

Jack and Diane

Jack married Diane in 2004. They separated in 2007, but grew closer following Andy's conviction of manslaughter for his involvement in Sarah's death.

He was sentenced on his and Jo's wedding day.

Diane was devastated in February 2009 when her beloved husband Jack died. Jack had been ill for some time and hadn't wanted to tell her. Her only comfort was a letter he'd written before his death, letting her know how much he loved her.

9

THE DINGLES

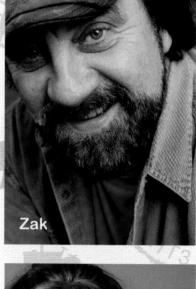

Zak

The Dingle clan is a very large one, with branches in Italy and Australia and no doubt many other countries. Wherever they live, every Dingle is up to something. For generations, there have been Dingles in Emmerdale, but other family members are always showing up to cause trouble. It's often tricky to work out which Dingles are siblings and which are cousins, and if some of the dates don't add up … well, the Dingles are always a bit vague when it comes to numbers.

Jeb (d 2002) and Peg Dingle had seven sons: Caleb, ZAK, Shadrach, Albert, Ezra, Obadiah and a seventh son whose name we don't know.

Zak (b 1952) is the patriarch of the Emmerdale Dingles, and was born in the village. He married Nellie, and had four children: Ben (1974-94) who died in a fight with Luke McAllister, SAM (b 1977), Tina (b 1977) and Butch (1972-2000).

Lisa

Nellie eventually got fed up of Zak and left him, and he went on to meet LISA (b 1956). They have a daughter, TINKERBELLE (b 1998), who everyone calls Belle and who was born on Christmas Day. Lisa hadn't realised she was pregnant.

Sam met Alice, a woman dying of cancer. They had a son, SAMSON (b 2006).

Caleb is older than Zak. He moved down to Southampton when he was young, and had a daughter, Mandy, who married the village vet PADDY, but ended up walking out on him.

Butch

Ben

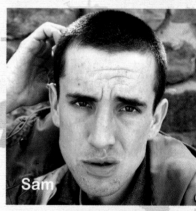

Sam

Tina

Belle

Alice & Samson

Shadrach

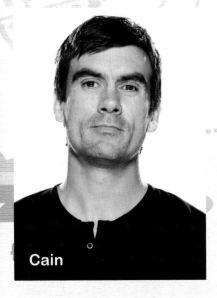

Cain

Chastity & Aaron

Marlon

Shadrach (1945 - 2010) was married to Faith and they had a daughter, CHASTITY (b 1977) who has a son, AARON (b 1992). Faith had a son, CAIN (b 1974) but the father was actually Zak. Shadrach was also the father of GENESIS ('Gennie') WALKER, whose mother was Shirley Pascoe, and who died giving birth to her.

A fourth brother, Albert, married Delilah and had two sons. MARLON (b 1974) married Tricia Stokes, but she died. He then married Donna Windsor. His younger brother Eli lived in Emmerdale for several years.

A fifth brother, Ezra, married Gwen and we don't know much about them except they have a son and a daughter.

A sixth brother, Obadiah, had a daughter, CHARITY (b 1978). Cousins Charity and Cain had a daughter when Charity was young, DEBBIE (b 1989). Debbie became a teenage mother herself, when she had her daughter with Andy Sugden, SARAH (b 2005). After an affair with his sister, Zoe, Charity married Chris Tate and had a son, NOAH (b 2004).

We don't know the name of the seventh Dingle brother, but by a process of elimination, he has to be the father of Del Dingle who lived in the village for a while, and her elder sister Lilith, who has four young children: Matthew, Mark, Luke and (a daughter) Jon who she once foisted on Marlon and Donna.

Tricia

Delilah

Charity

Debbie

VIV (b 1956) and Vic Windsor had both been married before, and each had a child from their first marriage. They came up from London to the Yorkshire Dales looking for a quiet life. Things didn't work out that way. Viv had a torrid affair with TERRY WOODS. Vic was later killed in a raid on the Post Office in 1998, while the rest of the family were enjoying Christmas dinner.

Viv

Vic

Scott

THE HOPES & WINDSORS

Scott is Viv's son, Kelly is Vic's daughter. Both had busy love lives and frequently embarked on reckless affairs. Kelly had a relationship with her teacher; Scott was kicked out of the army for seducing an officer's wife. Scott and Kelly even had an affair with each other. With so many enemies in the village, both have now moved away.

Kelly

The Windsor family, 1999

Vic and Viv had a daughter together, Donna. After relationships with Robert Sugden and Danny Daggert, Donna married Marlon Dingle and joined the police, having an affair with workmate Ross Kirk. When Marlon found out, Donna left Emmerdale.

Donna

Bob

In 2001, Viv married her third husband, salesman BOB HOPE (b 1960). Although he didn't tell Viv at first, Bob had recently been divorced from Clarissa and had two young children, Emma and Oliver. It didn't end there: he'd previously married Jean (twice), and had two kids Dawn (who came to the village and was briefly married to Viv's old flame Terry) and Jamie. He had Josh and Carly with his second wife, Barbara. He was married to a dancer called Vonda, but only for a day. Vonda had their daughter, Roxy.

Marlon

Bob with twins Heathcliff & Cathy

Viv divorced Bob, they remarried in 2006 but their relationship has again hit the rocks. They now have twins, HEATHCLIFF and CATHY, but all hope of a reunion has gone.

13

Bernice

THE BLACKSTOCKS

Bernice Blackstock first arrived in the village as a temporary barmaid, but Alan Turner hired her as the bar manager. She set about lording it over the two barmaids, Mandy Dingle and Alan's granddaughter, Tricia.

Her mother, DIANE (nee Lambert, b 1947) soon followed her to Emmerdale. Bernice and the village vicar, ASHLEY THOMAS (b 1961) came to realise they loved each other. As they planned their wedding, Ashley contacted Bernice's estranged father, RODNEY (b 1949), who arrived in the village much to Bernice and Diane's horror. Rodney had been a philanderer, who'd abandoned them. Ashley and Bernice married on Christmas Day 2000.

Ashley Thomas

Bernice learned she had a half-sister, Rodney's daughter NICOLA (b 1978). Both of them fell for Carlos, the hunky new chef at the Woolpack. Nicola got engaged to Carlos, Bernice became pregnant and wasn't sure if the father was Ashley or Carlos. This all became public knowledge on what was meant to be the day of Nicola and Carlos' wedding – which Ashley was officiating. Nicola left the village.

Bernice's baby, GABBY (b 2001) was born on her first wedding anniversary, and tests proved Ashley was the baby's father. After failing to make their marriage work, Bernice abandoned her husband and daughter in 2002, and has only returned to the village once since then.

Rodney

Diane

Gabby

Val

Diane's younger sister VAL (b 1953) also came to Emmerdale, and did little to smooth the waters with Diane when she quickly had an affair with Rodney. It was revealed that the two of them had seen each other behind Diane's back, many years before when Diane and Rodney were married and when Val was living with a man called Jimmy Pepper. Rodney was the father of Val's son, PAUL (b 1974). Val also had a daughter with Jimmy, Sharon, who has also shown up in the village a couple of times. Val has married the (equally) devious ERIC POLLARD.

Nicola returned in 2007, married to an elderly millionaire, Donald Da Souza, but when he died she didn't inherit the fortune she'd been expecting. Now she's settled down with JIMMY KING (b 1965), they're married, they have a daughter, ANGELICA (b 2009) and they're the new owners of The Woolpack.

Ashley moved on and married LAUREL Potts. They had a child, Daniel, who died of cot death syndrome after a few months, but the subsequent tests revealed that there had been a mix up at the hospital, and they'd been sent home with the wrong baby. Ashley sued for custody of the surviving boy, ARTHUR. Ashley's reprobate father, SANDY moved in with his son.

Diane married Jack Sugden, and has done her best to look after his children since his death.

Laurel

Nicola

Sandy

Jack and Diane

Jimmy King

2010 Highlights

The big story was Natasha Wylde shooting her husband Mark and burying his body in the woods. For months, the body lay there undisturbed, until it was discovered by Sam Dingle. While some villagers had been suspicious, most people accepted Natasha's story that Mark had just walked out on the family.

The police quickly established that Mark had been shot, so this was a case of murder – but who would they arrest for the crime, and how far would Natasha go to make sure it wasn't her?

Eventually Ryan was the one arrested and charged with Mark's murder.

Nathan had framed him in revenge for Faye and Ryan destroying his family's life.

After drugging Ashley, raping him, then leading him to think she was pregnant with his baby, deranged Emmerdale resident Sally Spode finally got her comeuppance.

Ashley's long-suffering wife, Laurel, decided to wreak her revenge, tracking down Sally to a block of flats outside the village.

Laurel threatened to throw Sally off the balcony, but the struggle ended and Sally was arrested.

Have we finally seen the last of Sally?

Diane Sugden was left penniless after her fiancé, Charlie Haynes, scammed her out of her life savings. Diane was forced to sell The Woolpack to Jimmy and Nicola King.

Whether Diane will return to Emmerdale one day remains to be seen.

Convinced that Aaron had returned to drug dealing, Paddy discovered that the bar Aaron was frequenting was, in fact, a gay bar. When confronted, the teenager lashed out and attacked him.

Still in denial, Aaron punched Jackson when he touched his arm in The Woolpack and he was charged with assault.

When Aaron realised that Marlon and Chas also knew about his true sexuality, he attempted suicide.

2010 Highlights

Jimmy King married Nicola, and they bought The Woolpack. Nicola loves the idea of being at the centre of the social life of the village, but does she really have the skills to run a pub and restaurant? And is Jimmy King really going to be happy running a pub in a small village when he was once heir-apparent to a sprawling business?

Eve Jenson returned for the first time in nearly five years. Previously, she'd been portrayed by the actress Raine Davison (daughter of *Doctor Who* actor Peter Davison). Now Eve is back, she's played by Suzanne Shaw, who used to be a member of the pop group Hear'Say, but who since then has built a career in West End musicals.

Hazel Walsh, mother of Jackson, arrived in the village in the summer. She's played by Pauline Quirke, still best-known as Sharon in the BBC sitcom *Birds of a Feather.*

Perhaps the strangest story happened off screen – it was widely reported that rap star P Diddy is a big fan of the show. This is not all that surprising: in the past, Johnny Depp and Wayne Rooney have said they're keen viewers. What makes P Diddy stand out is that the stories claim he's asked his agent to see if he can get a part in the show. Stay tuned!

2010 Highlights

A FAMILY AFFAIR

Self-made millionaires MARK and NATASHA WYLDE bought Home Farm, as well as the village church, ready to expand their business empire. They brought two sons, NATHAN and WILL, and a daughter, MAISIE.

EMMERDALE

What Natasha didn't know was that Mark was still married to his first wife, FAYE LAMB, who had a son, RYAN. Despite Natasha's attempts to pay them off, Faye and Ryan moved to Emmerdale and re-established contact with Mark. Faye and Mark were becoming close again. Natasha tolerated this as long as no one else in the village knew their secret.

When Ryan started dating Maisie, Mark and Natasha had to intervene and tell them they were half-siblings. Mark stormed out from the resulting family argument, with a shotgun. Natasha followed, but listening to Mark made her so angry she shot him. She buried him in the woods, and told the children her husband had abandoned them.

NEW KIDS ON THE BLOCK

JAI and NIKHIL SHARMA are entrepreneurial brothers who moved to Emmerdale to set up a sweet factory – Sharma and Sharma – that's proved to be an important local employer. Their sister, Priya worked at the factory, but got bored of the country life and soon left. Jai has started a romance with his PA, Faye Lamb.

THE SHARMA BROTHERS

JACKSON WALSH & HAZEL RHODES

JACKSON WALSH is a young gay man who's helped Aaron Livesy come to terms with his sexuality. He's moved to Emmerdale, where he works as a builder. His mother, HAZEL, has recently joined him there.

THE BARTON FAMILY

THE BARTONS are a farming family who have taken over the old Sugden Farm, now known as Butler Farm. They are John Barton, his wife Moira and their children Adam, Holly and Hannah. Moira works as a barmaid in The Woolpack. Holly dated Aaron Livesy, but Adam was convinced her boyfriend was gay. Holly has a more serious problem: she's become a regular user of cocaine.

ALICIA GALLAGHER

EMMERDALE

ALICIA GALLAGHER is the sister of Leyla Gallagher and has recently moved to the village...

DECLAN MACEY

DECLAN MACEY is a businessman who has bought a share in the Home Farm business and moved to the village. His affair with Natasha Wylde can only end in tears.

WOOLPACK GOSSIP

The centre of the social life of Emmerdale is The Woolpack pub. In the seventies and eighties, and for long before, it was run by Amos Brearley, who resisted even the most minor changes. Amos once chased a customer out for daring to suggest the pub should sell packets of nuts. His business partnership with Mr Wilks proved to be a strong one, though.

There's actually another pub in Emmerdale, although we've rarely seen it. It used to be called The Malt Shovel, and was run by cantankerous Ernie Shuttleworth. In recent years, it has been rebranded as a trendy wine bar, Malt.

In the nineties the next landlord, Alan Turner, transformed The Woolpack into a thriving, modern pub that served wine and food – against the wishes of many of the regulars, like Seth, who'd been drinking there since the Second World War and liked things the way they were (Turner eventually placed a small brass plaque on the bar, marking Seth's usual spot).

Bernice Blackstock, her mother Diane and Diane's sister Val continued modernising the Woolpack, and the pub became a popular place for villagers to have an evening meal, cooked by Marlon Dingle. Nowadays, most families in Emmerdale wouldn't dream of having their Christmas dinner anywhere else.

The Woolpack is haunted! At least, that's what some of the villagers believe, although no one's very clear on who the ghost was or why they'd haunt the place. It's also subject to a gypsy curse, and once had a run of bad luck when its Feng Shui energy was reversed by Bernice.

The new owners, Nicola and Jimmy King, are in a prime position to hear all the village gossip. But they should be warned: over the years, plenty of drama has taken place in the Woolpack itself.

The pub received a direct hit on the night of the plane crash. Many villagers were buried in the rubble. Chris Tate was paralysed, and had to start using a wheelchair.

The Woolpack moved to its current premises in 1976, when the old building was found to be suffering from subsidence.

Alan Turner welcomed his long-lost daughter, Tricia, into his life. Within a week, she had accidentally started a fire which gutted the Woolpack – she and bar manager Terry had been fooling around, and a candle fell into a box of fireworks.

Many years later, high winds during a freak storm dislodged the Woolpack's chimney, and Tricia was hit and killed by the debris.

HAPPILY EVER AFTER?

Every year, Emmerdale sees its fair share of weddings ... and more than its fair share of weddings that are called off at the last minute, or which end in tears before the day is out.

2010 saw the wedding of Nicola Da Souza and Jimmy King. Both had been married before ... Nicola to the ailing millionaire Donald Da Souza; Jimmy to the scheming Sadie.

Both had also previously called off a wedding on the day itself. In 2001, Nicola learned that her fiancé Carlos had been having an affair with her sister, Bernice. Nicola had a secret of her own: she wasn't really having a baby, as she'd told Carlos.

Jimmy had been all set to marry Kelly Windsor in 2007, but both had their secrets, and it all came pouring out on the wedding day.

This time, though, they left nothing to chance. At first, everything went to plan ...

... Until Nicola saw toddler Cathy Hope biting her daughter Angelica. To teach Cathy that was the wrong thing to do, Nicola gave her a gentle bite back. Cathy's mother, Viv, was furious and called the police.

Nicola was all set to miss her wedding day, as she was sent to court in York. Viv had a last-minute change of heart, though, and dropped the charges.

Really last minute! Nicola is forced to change into her wedding dress in the courtroom toilets ...

... And then race across the cobbled streets of York in her wedding dress.

Back in Emmerdale, there's a funeral scheduled after Nicola and Jimmy's wedding, and if they don't make it down the aisle soon, there will be a coffin blocking their way.

Nicola discovers that her wedding car has been wheel-clamped.

But Nicola makes it back to the village in the nick of time.

The service goes ahead. Nicola and Jimmy are married. The rest of the day goes without a hitch.

But will they live happily every after?

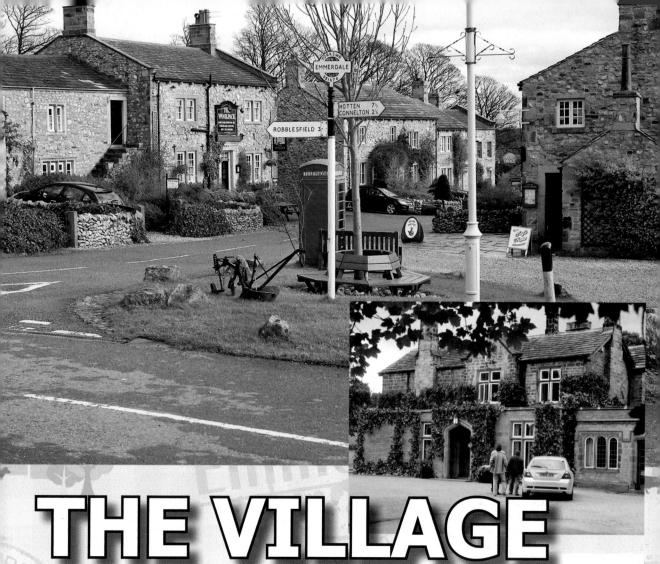

THE VILLAGE

Emmerdale is a small village in Yorkshire. It is 39 miles from Bradford and 52 miles from Leeds, in the Yorkshire Dales National Park, but doesn't appear on many maps. If you want to find it, set out from Hotten and it's about halfway between Connelton and Robblesfield.

Emmerdale sits on the banks of the River Emm. A bridge has stood there for centuries. On 30 December 1993, there was a terrible plane crash when a passenger jet exploded over the village. The bridge was blocked, which meant ambulances and fire engines couldn't reach survivors until villagers managed to improvise a new crossing.

Around three hundred people live in Emmerdale. There are two streets, Main Street and Church Lane, both off the main Robblesfield Road.

Emmerdale village is at the bottom of a steep hill called The Struggle. Nearly all the houses in Emmerdale are built from grey Yorkshire sandstone, with blue/grey slate roofs. There are several dozen houses, and other buildings including a church that's been the victim of arson twice in recent years, a village hall, a vicarage, a sweet factory, a post office and shop, a vet's surgery and a cricket pavilion.

There are a number of cottages, all with their own names – these include Pear Tree Cottage, Woodbine Cottage (where Edna Birch lives), Tug Ghyll, Dale Head Farm, Mill Cottage, Mill Brook (the largest house in the village itself), Keeper's Cottage (where Betty lives), Victoria Cottage, Dale View and Jacob's Fold. The oldest building in Emmerdale is Tenant House, built in 1671, also known as Annie's Cottage.

The graveyard contains monuments to the villagers who've died over the years, from the elaborate headstone for Frank Tate through to a small wooden cross for Ben Dingle.

The Dingle homestead, Wishing Well Cottage, and the much posher Holdgate's Farm are adjacent properties, about five hundred yards outside the village.

Emmerdale Farm, the former home of the Sugden family, is further away but within easy walking distance.

Home Farm, the centre of the largest local estate, is a little further away and most villagers with business there tend to drive.

The nearest railway station, supermarket and secondary school are all in Hotten. There's a regular bus service from Emmerdale.

THE LOVES OF CAIN DINGLE

When he arrived in Emmerdale, troublemaker Cain Dingle caught the eye of young Ollie Reynolds. It was her mother, Angie, who Cain wanted, even though she was a policewoman and the Dingles traditionally try to keep as far from possible from the police. After months of flirting, Cain and Angie began an affair, but Angie soon realised she'd made a mistake. Cain did not take rejection kindly – he got Angie fired, seduced Ollie and threw Angie's elderly father Len down the stairs. Despite all that, Angie couldn't stay away from Cain – dying in his arms when a robbery they planned together went wrong.

OLLIE

ANGIE

CHARITY

Cain always had the hots for his cousin Charity Dingle. Although Charity had kept quiet about it, when she was very young, they'd had a daughter together, Debbie. When Charity moved to Emmerdale, she had her sights firmly set on millionaire Chris Tate. They married, but Charity soon succumbed to Cain's charms. Chris learned he was dying, and decided to take revenge on his wife, making his death look like murder. Coincidentally, Cain had actually been planning to murder Chris, but it was Charity who went to jail.

When Charity was released, she decided she liked the lifestyle she'd had with Chris, and planned to marry the wealthy Tom King. Tom's daughter-in-law, Sadie, hired Cain to ruin the wedding. Those plans backfired and Sadie was disowned by her family. She ended up spending one night with Cain, before realising how dangerous he was when he killed her dog Damon. Charity fled the village.

Debbie Dingle fell in love with Jasmine Thomas, and Cain disapproved. He split them up by seducing Jasmine.

JASMINE

Sadie hired Cain to do her dirty work again, and this led to a show home Jimmy King had built being destroyed, killing the people inside. Sadie refused to renew her relationship with Cain, but when he tried to hurt her by revealing all her secrets, she simply told the Dingles how he had betrayed Debbie. Forced out of the Dingle clan, Cain left Emmerdale for a while.

MAISIE

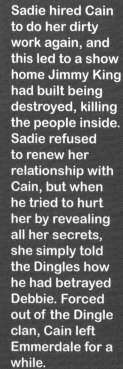

In 2009, Cain returned to the village to look after Debbie. He flirted with Maisie Wylde, but was more interested in Faye Lamb. Cain came to see that Faye was using him to make her ex-husband Mark jealous.

FAYE

SADIE

By this time, Debbie was in a relationship with a man called Michael, but she and Cain learned Michael was getting married to someone else. They crashed the wedding, and were shocked to discover that the bride-to-be was Charity. Michael didn't know that Charity had a daughter, that she'd been married before, or about any of the other scandalous things she'd done. He left her, and Debbie. Furious with Cain for ruining her life again, Charity nevertheless had to admit she was attracted to him. After a furious row, she proposed to him on Christmas Day 2009.

HEROES & VILLAINS

In Emmerdale, as in life, people change over time, and good people occasionally do bad things for what they think are the right reasons. Andy Sugden has gone from being a child with a troubled upbringing but a heart of gold, through to a man who hit his own wife (and who accidentally killed his adopted mother).

Everyone in the village is suspicious of the Dingles, and it's probably best to keep your valuables close by when they're around ... but are Zak and Sam Dingle really more wicked than the outwardly-respectable Tates, Kings or Wyldes? It can't be a coincidence that the most ruthless Dingles, Cain and Charity, often find themselves intimately involved with the people up at Home Farm.

That said, there are some real villains in Emmerdale.

Sally Spode was an old flame of Ashley who came to the village intent on causing harm to his wife Laurel. She let an ember from a November 5th bonfire catch light on Laurel's coat and did nothing. Later, she trapped Laurel in the village hall and set fire to it. The villagers came to realise she was dangerous. She kidnapped Edna's dog and trashed Terry Woods' house. Laurel confronted Sally at Sally's flat – which was a shrine to Ashley. After a tense confrontation, Sally was arrested and sectioned under the Mental Health Act.

Eric Pollard has lived in Emmerdale for over twenty years, and in that time he's swindled and cheated just about everyone in the village. Always bitter that he doesn't get the recognition he deserves, Pollard has sold his – and others' – stories to the tabloids. He probably killed his wife Elizabeth during the plane crash (although nothing was ever proved). He schemed with his third wife, Gloria, to gain political power, but in the end she double-crossed him and went off to become an MP in Westminster herself.

But there are also good people in the village.

Terry Woods isn't perfect, but he's an honest man, a good friend and he's had more than his share of misfortune. He's been a confidant to a lot of people in the village, but he's been very unlucky in love.

Ashley Thomas, the local vicar, has a little bit of a ruthless streak when he's pushed, but doesn't display it all that often – usually when people try to take advantage of him, or vulnerable villagers. He's a good man, though, and everyone in the village trusts him.

Edna Birch may not be the nicest or most charming person in the village, but she's a genuinely good woman. She defends her friends, believes in them when no one else does. She tries to protect the young people of the village and, although she's got a strict faith, her advice is usually very practical. Edna is devoted to her dogs.

FAVOURITE MOMENTS

Emmerdale is hugely popular now, known for its sensational storylines. It's been running since 1972, and fans of the show fondly remember characters and events of the past.

In 1977, the villagers celebrated the Queen's Silver Jubilee with a street party.

The early eighties saw Alan Turner running NY Estates, up at Home Farm. Joe Sugden worked for him and was keen to make money from agriculture, but often found himself clashing with Turner's methods.

Seth was always up to something, usually a way to get something for nothing. Particularly if that was a free pint at the Woolpack. Whether the landlord was Amos, Turner or Bernice, it made no difference.

Kathy Tate was the village sweetheart, but was often the victim of people around her. That said, Kathy managed to survive four marriages and several murder attempts.

Frank Tate brought a new, entrepreneurial spirit to Home Farm, not to mention a sexy young second wife, Kim, who could match him in every way. Eventually, she faked her own death and returned, giving Frank a heart attack. Watching her husband die, Kim paused only to adjust her lipstick before seizing the reigns of power.

Zoe Tate, Frank's daughter, was a successful vet. She came out as a lesbian, and enjoyed many years as a favourite of villagers and viewers. She was a Tate, though, and had an affair with her brother's fiancée, Charity.

Lady Tara was only in the village for a couple of years, but her combination of beauty, wealth and her desire to get what she wanted without worrying too much about hurting those below her proved irresistible.

Tricia Stokes and Bernice battled constantly in The Woolpack, both trying to upstage and humiliate the other in their efforts to impress Tricia's grandfather, Turner. They eventually became firm friends.

FAVOURITE MOMENTS

Hunky John Barton and his vivacious wife Moira took over the running of the farm from the Sugden family. The couple have three children - Adam, Holly and Hannah.

When Jack's wife Sarah cheated on him, Diane was there with a shoulder to cry on. Their friendship grew over the years and the couple eventually married in September 2004.

After an absence of four years, Charity Dingle returned in October 2009 when Debbie Dingle gatecrashed her lover's wedding to find that his intended bride was Charity, her mother.

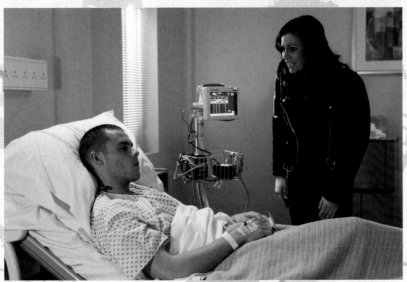

On awakening in hospital after his failed suicide attempt, Aaron finds renewed support from Chas and Adam. Later, in court, Aaron finally finds the courage to admit that he is gay.

HEADLINE QUIZ

Can you fill in the names missing from these Hotten Courier headlines? Answers on page 61.

1   POLICEWOMAN GRACE ⬚ DIES IN LORRY 'ACCIDENT'

2   THREE KILLED IN GAS EXPLOSION AT KING ⬚

3   ⬚ AND LORRY COLLIDE IN EMMERDALE MAIN STREET

4   SHARMA AND SHARMA OPEN NEW ⬚ FACTORY

5   SHOCKED DEBBIE – 'I CAUGHT MY FELLA MARRYING MY ⬚'

6   JACOB SUGDEN DIES, ⬚ SUGDEN INHERITS EMMERDALE FARM

7   HEADMISTRESS DEATH VERDICT: MARC REYNOLDS FOUND ⬚

8   WOOLPACK FIRE RESULT OF MISHAP WITH ⬚

9   ⬚ 'COMES BACK FROM THE DEAD'

10   ⬚ KING SHOT, SURVIVES

THE KING DYNASTY

Whoever owns Home Farm controls Emmerdale. Home Farm itself is a manor house, and not a particularly large one, but it comes with many hundreds of acres of valuable farmland as well as associated property and business interests that have varied over time, but included a holiday village, a trout farm, a haulage company and many rental properties and tenant farms. The Home Farm estate is the biggest employer in the Emmerdale area. Over the years, it's belonged to many families, including the Verneys, the Oakwells and the Tates. A powerful businessman or businesswoman with firm control of the reins of Home Farm is onto a surefire winner … if they can avoid disaster and distractions.

Tom King grew up modestly in Emmerdale during the forties. He moved away, but as he became a wealthy man, he had a very strong nostalgia for the village, and set his sights on buying Home Farm. He had four sons, Jimmy, Matthew, Carl and Max. All of them savvy businessmen, but none as ruthless as Jimmy's wife Sadie. Jimmy saw himself as the person who'd one day inherit his father's business, but Tom gave Sadie the most crucial jobs.

Matthew King was jealous of the attention Jimmy and Sadie got from Tom, and worked hard to prove himself. Keeping her options open, Sadie had an affair with her brother-in-

law. Carl King was ambitious, but not favoured by his father. He became involved with Chas Dingle. Max was the only brother who didn't work for the company, he worked as a vet. He was killed in a car crash.

Charity Tate quickly seduced Tom, and they got engaged. Sadie did everything she could to sabotage the wedding, which duly ended in disaster. Charity ended up in an affair with Jimmy, and when this was exposed by Sadie, she countered by showing the full extent of Sadie's own scheming, and Sadie was forced to leave the village.

Carl, Jimmy and Matthew cover up the death of Paul Marsden, who'd died in a roofing accident.

BK 44 569821 3

HOTTEN POLICE DEPARTMENT

25.12.06

KING . CARL

Tom King finally managed to buy Home Farm, but Zoe Tate had her revenge and seriously damaged the building in an explosion.

On the day Tom King was due to marry Rosemary Sinclair, Christmas Day 2006, he was murdered when someone pushed him through a window. The police investigation began, and there was no shortage of people who might have wanted Tom dead.

After months, Carl confessed to his brothers that he'd killed their father. He began dating Grace Barraclough, the policewoman who was investigating Tom's murder. She was suspicious of him, but before she could prove anything she was killed when a lorry hit her. The King brothers had got away with murder …

… Then Rosemary Sinclair vanished, and Matthew was convicted of her killing. He was sent to jail … but she was alive. A year to the day after Tom died, she reappeared in the village, but by the end of the day she had shot herself.

Kelly Windsor seduced Jimmy, and he soon proposed. Once again, the wedding did not take place when both of them realised the other had a dark secret.

THE KING DYNASTY

During the course of 2008, Carl and Jimmy both survived being shot. Matthew's wedding to Anna Da Souza also ended in tears, with Matthew and Carl fighting each other. Matthew tried to run Carl over in a van, but ended up killing himself when the van hit a wall.

One day later, the King business empire lies in tatters and the Kings have to leave Home Farm.

Carl's wife Lexi left the village after he admitted that he didn't love her. Carl is reunited with Chas Dingle and they are trying to settle down, despite the attentions of Eve Jenson.

Jimmy is now married to Nicola and they own The Woolpack.

Home Farm is now owned by the Wyldes, and Natasha Wylde has already murdered her husband.

WORDSEARCH

Can you find the names of 10 people or families associated with Emmerdale? Remember, the words could be concealed in any direction!

```
J  G  T  E  R  R  Y  W  O  O  D  S
V  N  T  Z  W  V  N  D  K  G  W  N
K  E  E  B  X  K  C  C  K  I  M  L
J  L  L  D  D  R  A  L  L  O  P  M
A  G  N  C  G  D  Y  L  X  B  Q  E
I  N  M  O  T  U  W  M  M  P  P  B
S  I  T  L  A  Y  S  A  M  O  R  L
H  D  N  W  L  H  L  T  H  K  B  G
A  K  L  D  R  E  T  V  R  X  G  M
R  A  E  B  Y  F  I  A  Y  J  N  M
M  Z  Y  A  W  V  J  N  T  P  I  J
A  B  F  J  G  K  R  X  R  E  K  X
```

ZAK DINGLE   JAI SHARMA   KING
VIV HOPE   WILL WYLDE   FAYE LAMB
TERRY WOODS   POLLARD
NOAH TATE   SUGDEN

Answers on Page 61

43

GONE...
but not forgotten

Frank & Kim

Chris

Over the years, many colourful characters have lived in Emmerdale. Eventually there comes a time when they leave, sometimes in triumph, but more often in tragedy.

The Tate dynasty once ruled Emmerdale. In the early nineties, FRANK TATE, a colourful entrepreneur bought the stately manor, Home Farm and every decision he made had an impact on village life. His young second wife, KIM schemed to keep control of Frank's empire away from his children, CHRIS and ZOE. Frank died of a heart attack. Chris, in a wheelchair following the plane crash, and Kim battled over the business empire. Kim stole millions, left Chris for dead and fled the village in a helicopter, never to be seen again.

Zoe

CHARITY DINGLE and Chris would later marry, and his new wife would prove just as manipulative and keen to cling on to Home Farm. Chris learned she had betrayed him and made his death from a terminal illness look like murder – a crime Charity was accused of. In the end, it was mild-mannered ZOE who took revenge, burning down Home Farm as she left Emmerdale.

SETH ARMSTRONG was Emmerdale's oldest and most recognisable resident. He lived his whole life in the village, and spent every evening for sixty years drinking in The Woolpack (although rarely paid for his own drinks). Everyone in the village liked him and listened to his advice, and no one could match his local knowledge. He was married for a long time to Meg, and after she died Seth was reunited with his childhood sweetheart, Betty Eagleton, the childless widow of Wally Eagleton.

Seth

GONE...
but not forgotten

Joe

Annie

Jack

JACK SUGDEN inherited the family farm in 1972. For twenty years after that, he and his younger brother JOE constantly clashed over the best way to run a modern farm. Joe grew depressed after the plane crash and moved to Spain with his mother, ANNIE SUGDEN. He died there in a car crash. Fifteen years later, Jack was visiting Spain when he suffered declining health and a fatal heart attack.

Annie, the matriarch of the family and a formidable presence, survived both her sons. She returned to Emmerdale in 1995 and 2009, to bury them in the village.

SHADRACH DINGLE had always had a drinking problem, and in 2010 it was this that finally killed him. Diagnosed with serious liver problems, he didn't give up the booze. He fell into a river in a drunken stupor, while trying to retrieve beer cans he'd dropped.

Shadrach

Amos & Henry

The older residents – and viewers – of Emmerdale fondly remember AMOS BREARLY and HENRY WILKS. Amos and Mr Wilks were the bickering business partners who owned The Woolpack for many, many years.

WHERE'S BELLE?

Can you spot Belle Dingle in the crowd below?
If you're stumped, you can find out where she is on Page 60.

48

CROSSWORD

Read the clues, fill in the relevant spaces and see if you can complete the crossword!

ACROSS

1 Village pub (3,8)
5 The nearest big town to Emmerdale (6)
6 Bernice, Diane and Rodney _____ (10)
10 Emmerdale is in this part of the world (9)
11 Zak's first wife (6)
13 Ashley's job (5)
15 Cain pushed him down the stairs (3)
18 Scott was a _____ (7)
19 Emmerdale is a _____ Opera (4)

DOWN

2 Pollard's first name (4)
3 Actor who played Sadie King (5,6)
4 Father of Andy, Robert and Victoria (4,6)
6 Francis Dingle was better known as _____ (5)
7 Was 1 Across's oldest customer (4)
8 Drink served at 1 Across (3)
9 Batley and Damon were _____ (4)
12 This river flows through Emmerdale (3)
14 Grumpy old landlord of 1 Across (4)
16 Paddy's surname (4)
17 Zak's second wife (4)

Answers on Page 61

DID YOU KNOW?
10 Facts About Cast Members

The longest-serving actor now is Richard Thorp, who plays Alan Turner. He's worked on the show since 1982. He started work on the show on his fiftieth birthday.

The longest-serving female cast member is now Deena Payne (Viv Hope). Viv's been on our screens since 1993.

The actor who plays Terry Woods, Billy Hartman, is Scottish, and played Duncan Macleod's cousin, a Dark Ages Scottish warrior, in *Highlander*.

Sian Reese-Williams, who plays Gennie Walker, is from Brecon, and speaks Welsh at home.

Chris Chittell, who plays Eric Pollard, was a regular in the seventies SF show *The Tomorrow People*.

Tony Audenshaw, who plays Bob Hope, ran the 2010 London Marathon dressed as a baby and completed the race in 3 hours, 13 minutes.

In an episode of sixties spy-fi series *The Avengers,* Patrick Mower (Rodney Blackstock) played a sinister history student with an evil plan to introduce a single European currency.

Paula Tillbrook, who plays Betty Eagleton, was once Speaker of the House of Commons … in the television series *To Play the King.*

Natalie J Robb (Moira Barton) has also been a regular character in soaps *Take the High Road, Dream Team, The Bill, Doctors* and *EastEnders.*

Channel 4 placed Amanda Donahue (Natasha Wylde) 38th in their list of 50 Greatest British Actresses, between Claire Bloom and Thandie Newton. Barbara Windsor was 33rd and Tilda Swinton was 44th.

BEHIND THE SCENES

There are six new episodes of Emmerdale shown every week, and it's a huge amount of work to make that much television. There are around fifty regular members of cast, and a small army of people behind the cameras.

The vast majority of scenes are filmed on one of two sites – a large purpose-built studio in the middle of Leeds and the 300-acre village set about twenty five minutes' drive away. Most, but not all, of the scenes set inside are recorded in the studio. Usually one crew is filming at the village, another in the studio, making different blocks of episodes – it can mean that actors have to be whisked from one to the other.

If you see a scene set outside, it's filmed at the village set. When you see a character outside going into The Woolpack, then see him at the bar, the two scenes were filmed at locations ten miles apart, and almost certainly on different days.

The Emmerdale studio is one of the biggest television studios in the country, half the size of a soccer pitch, all of it dedicated to one show. Here, the sets for the interior of the Woolpack, Home Farm, the Post Office and all the various cottages and houses stand back-to-back.

Downstairs are the make-up rooms, the wardrobe department, the editing suites, the canteen and the dressing rooms.

Upstairs is the production office, where Emmerdale is planned. A team of storyliners, researchers, writers and script editors put together the scripts, then another team plans out how to turn what's on the page into television – booking directors and guest actors, devising props and hiring any special equipment … even finding stuntmen.

This is all very impressive, but the showpiece for Emmerdale is the village itself. It's a 300-acre site designed to look like a genuine Yorkshire village. It is the largest permanent television set in the world.

The original designer, Mike Long, wanted to give the directors total freedom to explore the village, shoot it from any angle. If you were dropped into the middle of the village, it would take you a little while to realise it wasn't genuine. You can walk up and down the streets, explore round the backs of the houses. You can go up to the bus stop and read what time the bus to Hotten is running, or to the Woolpack and check the menu.

The chimneys have smoke canisters in them to make it look like people have their fires burning.

This year, the Emmerdale village was closed for a few days because of heavy snow – while filming was impossible, it gave the crew an opportunity to take some very pretty pictures.

The Emmerdale village is very cleverly designed, though – many of the buildings are used to store equipment and props, and as dressing rooms.

DISASTERS

Emmerdale is a small village, but it attracts catastrophe. The disasters can be man-made or natural, personal tragedy or devastation that impacts every single person in the village. Emmerdale is a tight-knit community, so whoever dies or ends up critically-injured in hospital, there are always plenty of people directly affected by the loss of a loved one, a business partner or someone who shares their darkest secrets.

In 1993, a plane crashed on the village of Beckindale, as it was then known, leaving most buildings seriously damaged and killing many people on the ground.

Alan Turner's wife, Shirley, was killed in an armed raid on Home Farm a year later.

Dave Glover was killed in a fire at Home Farm. He'd been having an affair with the lady of the manor, Kim Tate. Kim had just had baby James, who may have been his. When smoke filled James' nursery, it was Dave who rushed in to save him … and who died from smoke inhalation.

Seemingly mild-mannered schoolteacher Graham Clark had killed his first wife before moving to the village. He threw Rachel Hughes off a cliff when she worked out what he'd done. A year later he was engaged to Kathy, and she also figured it out … this time, it was Graham who fell to his death.

A lorry from Tate Haulage and a bus crashed in the middle of the village, killing the lorry driver, Pete Collins and Butch Dingle, and injuring many others.

Sarah Sugden was killed when Andy burned down a barn for the insurance money, not realising his mother was trapped inside.

In 2001, a group of school kids from Emmerdale stole a car and accidentally hit and killed their headmistress, Miss Strickland. The car was driven by Marc Reynolds, and although they vowed to keep quiet, it was inevitable that the truth would come out. Marc was sent to prison.

DISASTERS

Zoe Tate, suffering from schizophrenia, burned down the village Church, and would later set off an explosion at Home Farm. A few years later, Sally Spode would burn the Church down again. Soon after that, the village vicar, Ashley, accidentally ran over Sally.

In winter 2004, a huge storm downed power lines and left many people stranded and vulnerable. Tricia Dingle was killed by falling masonry.

A gas leak at the King's show home set off a series of explosions that killed Noreen Bell, David Brown and Dawn Woods.

Douglas Potts, Leyla Harding and Ryan Lamb were all in the Home Farm Shop when a runaway vintage van crashed into the building. Mark Wylde came to the aid of the injured Ryan and was forced to admit that he was Ryan's father.

The BIG Quiz

How much do you know about Emmerdale and the people who live there? All the information you need is in this book somewhere, but if you still don't know then the answers are on page 61.

5

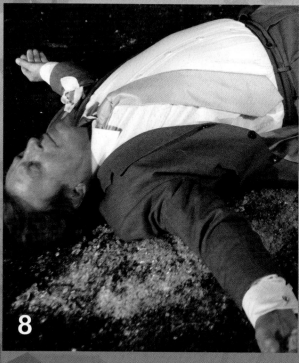

8

1 Which year did a plane crash on the village?

2 What do the following events have in common: Vic Windsor's murder, Ashley and Bernice get married, Bernice has baby Gabby, Rosemary Sinclair shoots herself?

3 Which Dingle is not Zak's son: Sam, Ben, Butch or Marlon?

4 How are Sarah Sugden and Sarah Sugden Jnr related?

5 How many wives has Bob Hope had?

6 There are two pubs in Emmerdale, name them.

7 What is the name of Sam's son?

8 Who killed Tom King?

9 How many daughters do Rodney, Zak and Charity have between them?

10 Diane, Charity, Zak and Betty are all grandparents. True or false?

AWARDS & ACCOLADES

The biggest reward for the people making Emmerdale is that audiences tune in for the next episode, day after day. It means the show is doing something right. It's always nice to get other forms of recognition, though. In recent years, Emmerdale has won a number of awards, some voted for by the public, some given to them by panels of television professionals and experts.

In early 2001, Emmerdale won a prestigious BAFTA for Best Continuing Drama, recognition of the strength of the show in 2000. The example of the show sent to the judges was the heartbreaking episode where Butch Dingle married Emily on his deathbed. The show was nominated again in 2007, 2008 and 2009.

Emmerdale has also done well in the British Soap Awards. In 2008, Emmerdale won two – Best Single Episode for the episode in which baby Daniel Thomas died, and director Tony Prescott won a Special Achievement Awards.

In 2010, long-serving Emmerdale writer Bill Lyons, who also helped create EastEnders, won a Special Achievement award.

Emmerdale has dominated the Spectacular Scene Award, winning in 2006 for Belle and Daz trapped in a mine shaft, 2007 for the show home collapse and 2009 when Victoria fell through the ice.

It also won Soap Awards for the Best Single Episode in 2005, Charity Tate's ruined wedding. The architect of Charity's misfortune was Sadie King, played by Patsy Kensit, but she missed out on the coveted Bitch of the Year award to Nicola Wheeler (Nicola Da Souza). Inside Soap gave their Best Bitch award to Kensit, though.

In 2007, Eden Taylor-Draper won Best Dramatic Performance from a Young Actor, for her work as Belle Dingle at the Soap Awards and also at the Inside Soap Awards.

The Dingle Family won Best Soap Family in 2006, Best Storyline for Alice Dingle's battles with cancer in 2007. Charlie Hardwick (Val Pollard) won Funniest Character the same year, and the following year, her on-screen husband, Chris Chittell, won an Outstanding Achievement Award for his work as Eric Pollard.

QUIZ ANSWERS

WHERE'S BELLE?

HEADLINE QUIZ

1 Barroclough
2 Show Home
3 Bus
4 Sweet
5 Mum
6 Jack
7 Guilty
8 Fireworks
9 Kim
10 Carl

WORDSEARCH

CROSSWORD

THE BIG QUIZ

1 1993 (December 30th)

2 They all happened on Christmas Day (of different years)

3 Marlon

4 Sarah Jnr is the daughter of Andy Sugden, Sarah Snr's adopted son

5 Five … he's had seven weddings, but married Jean and Viv twice

6 The Woolpack and Malt (formerly the Malt Shovel)

7 Samson

8 Carl King

9 Six (they each have two, that we know of)

10 False – Betty never had children.

HEARTTHROBS